PIERCE MIDDLE SCHOOL
25605 Orangelawn
Redford, MI 48239

D0811707

Our World

GRASSLANDS

David Lambert

Silver Burdett Press
Englewood Cliffs, New Jersey

Titles in this series

Coasts

Deserts

Grasslands

Jungles and Rainforests

Mountains

Polar Regions

Pollution and Conservation

Rivers and Lakes

Seas and Oceans

Temperate Forests

First published in 1987 by
Wayland (Publishers) Ltd
61 Western Road, Hove
East Sussex BN3 1JD. England

Adapted and first published in the
United States in 1988 by Silver Burdett Press,
Englewood Cliffs, New Jersey

© Copyright 1987 Wayland (Publishers) Ltd

© 1988 this adaptation Silver Burdett Press
All Rights Reserved

Editor: Rhoda Nottridge

U.S. edition edited by Nancy Furstinger

Series designer: Malcolm Smythe
Book designer: Ross George
Series consultant: Keith Lye

Typeset by DP Press, Sevenoaks, Kent
Printed in Italy by G. Canale & C.S.p.A., Turin

Library of Congress Cataloging-in-Publication Data

Lambert, David, 1932–
    Grasslands/David Lambert.
    p.   cm. — (Our world)
    Bibliography: p.
    Includes index.
    Summary: Explores different types of grasslands located around
the world, describing their development, climate, plant and animal
life, exploitation, and preservation.
    1. Grassland ecology – Juvenile literature.   2. Grasslands –
Juvenile literature.   [1. Grassland ecology.   2. Grasslands.
3. Ecology.]   I. Title.   II. Series.
QH541.5.P7L36 1988
574.5′2643–dc 19   88–18438 CIP   AC

ISBN 0-382-09789-0

Front cover, main picture A lion in African Savanna grassland.

Front cover, inset A coyote in North American grassland.

Back cover A baobab tree showing elephant damage in East Africa.

Contents

Oceans of grass

Imagine an ocean of grasses stretching as far as you can see. Among the grasses grow other soft-stemmed flowering plants. But there are only scattered trees or no trees at all.

Much natural grassland of this kind lies in the center of continents where the soil is too dry for a forest, but too moist for a desert. Here, most rain falls at one time of year. Then new leaves sprout and the land grows fresh and green. In the dry season, plants wither, the land turns dry and brown, and fires may sweep across the countryside.

Wild grasslands once covered perhaps one-third of all the earth's land. The two largest kinds of grasslands sprawl across vast flat or rolling plains. Temperate grasslands such as steppes and prairies lie roughly halfway between the equator and the poles, in climates that are neither hot nor cold. Tropical grasslands, or savannas, lie in belts of hot land on either side of the equator. Wild grassland also grows on moors and mountains, and people have covered many areas with grassland where forest used to stand. But this book is mainly about the world's grassy plains.

At one time, only wild plants, animals, and a few human hunter-gatherers inhabited the prairies and savannas. Each plant and creature was fitted to survive in just this kind of countryside. Then farmers and herders moved in with their crops and cattle. Today, huge areas of grassland have been plowed up and sown with food plants or been cultivated as pasture land. Such altered grasslands supply most of the world's grains. But this means that the many kinds of wild plants and animals are replaced by just a few domesticated species. In places, too, misuse of soil turns grasslands into deserts where not even crops or cattle thrive. However, people can repair this damage and save grassland soil and wildlife for the future.

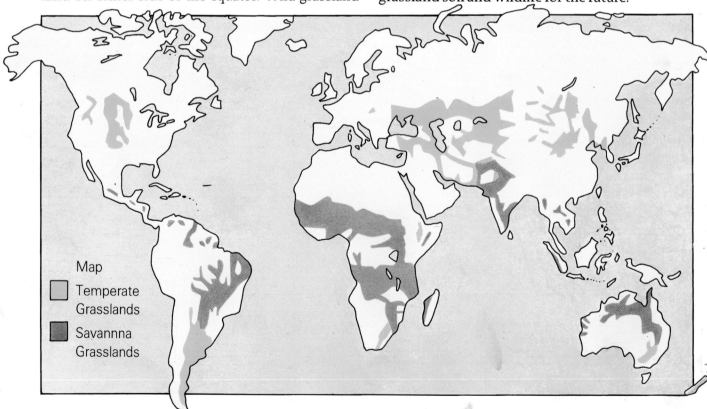

Map
Temperate Grasslands
Savannna Grasslands

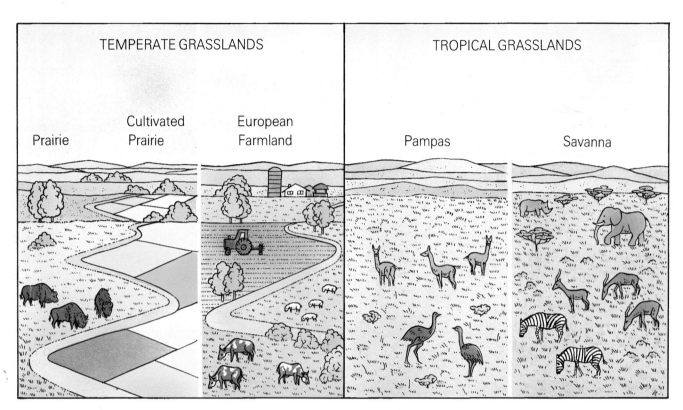

| TEMPERATE GRASSLANDS | | | TROPICAL GRASSLANDS | |
| Prairie | Cultivated Prairie | European Farmland | Pampas | Savanna |

Above This picture illustrates the different types of grassland.

Right A herd of wildebeest migrates across the East African savanna. The world's grasslands feed millions of grazing mammals.

Left This world map shows the main tropical grasslands (savannas) and temperate grasslands. Most lie in rather dry areas away from oceans.

How grasslands developed

There were no grasslands in the days of dinosaurs, more than 60 million years ago. Forests covered most parts of all continents. But by 35 million years ago the world climate changed and some forests started to disappear. One reason for climatic change was the growth of mountains. In North America the rising Rocky Mountains stopped moist winds from the Pacific Ocean from bringing rain to places far inland. These now had dry summers and even drier winters. As soil dried out, moisture-loving trees died off. Trees also died on land that cooled down as it rose to form the mountain tops.

Where trees disappeared, new kinds of plants that thrived in fairly dry or cool conditions began to take their place. The most successful of these plants were grasses.

Early grasslands were probably just clearings in the forests. But by five million years ago large parts of most continents were drying out or cooling down. So steppe and prairie grasses spread across

Mountains rising in western North America made the Midwest more suitable for growing grass than trees.

the middle of North America and Asia. Farther south, savanna grasses ate into the drying lands that rimmed the tropical forests of Africa and South America.

Drying climates helped create the world's first grasslands, but humans helped the grasslands to spread. Hunters of the Old Stone Age probably began burning forests to encourage grass to grow instead of trees. Grass nourished the animals these people killed for food – big, meaty grazing beasts like bison, antelopes, and horses. Later, herdsmen and shepherds regularly burned the land. Burning

A grass fire in Tanzania lights up the night sky. Fires have destroyed huge tracts of African forest and helped cover land with grass instead of trees.

encouraged growth of young tender grass on which their flocks and herds could graze. Then came the farmers with their axes. By 4,000 years ago farmers had begun chopping down the trees that covered much of Europe. Today sheep and cattle graze on meadows where forests once stood. Around the world, cultivated grasslands take up huge areas that would be forests if people let the trees grow again.

Where they lie

Temperate grasslands lie mainly in the dry hearts of continents, outside the tropics. Here, grasses are mostly shorter than tropical savanna grasses and there are usually fewer trees. Grass grows thickly in the moister places. However, the driest areas have only scattered clumps with bare soil between. Great belts of temperate grassland once covered plains and rolling hills on every continent except Antarctica. But farming and livestock raising have largely changed the vegetation.

The world's largest grassland is Eurasia's *steppe* – a Russian word for grassy plain. Steppe grassland once covered the vast plains that sprawl 2,500 miles from the western U.S.S.R. into Central Asia. West of the steppe, another grassy plain, the *puszta*, spreads across much of Hungary.

In North America the prairies once formed a sea of grass that filled the central lowlands between the Appalachian and Rocky Mountains. Grass grew thickly on the moist prairie of the east. But in the drier west it just formed scattered clumps.

South America's great temperate grassland is the *pampa*, meaning plain, of east-central Argentina, a region more than three times the size of Great Britain. North, east, and south, it fades out into drier land with scrubby vegetation.

Lush spring grass and brightly flowering plants form carpets on the moister plains of the United States.

Smaller areas of temperate grassland occur in South Africa, Australia, and New Zealand. South African grassland grows largely on uplands called *veld* (veld means field). Southeast Australia and New Zealand's South Island have grassy plains and hills called *downs*.

Around the world, belts of grass encircle mountains in the cool air above the tree line – even in the tropics. Rich meadows flourish on the European Alps. Coarse *patana* grassland grows on Sri Lanka's highlands. Tufted grassland thrives on tall East African volcanoes. Higher still are the coarse cushions of the South American *puna* and Central Asian *pamir* – grasslands on the highest plateaus in the world.

Below Cattle graze on sparse, dry, prairie grasses. This treeless tract lies in Montana.

Most western European grassland is artificial. In Great Britain, Germany, and France huge areas of forest have been cut down and now the land is used for growing cereals and creating grassland for grazing animals. In many Mediterranean areas, much of the grassland was originally scrubland which has been cultivated for thousands of years.

Natural European grasslands lie on the plains of Hungary and the Ukraine. The Ukrainian grassland, in the U.S.S.R., is part of the world's largest grassland and is called the Eurasian steppe. It stretches from Europe to China.

This grassy slope overlooks a valley in the Pamirs Central Asian highlands mainly in the U.S.S.R.

Weather and climate

The climates of temperate grasslands depend largely on their distance from the equator and oceans. The great grasslands of the northern hemisphere lie halfway between the equator and the North Pole. They also are deep inland. Land heats up and cools down faster than water. So in the summer, steppes and prairies grow hotter than the ocean shores that far north. But in wintertime they become far colder.

On the prairies, temperatures can soar above 100° F in the long sunny summer days, from June to August. But in winter, temperatures plunge. The average January temperature at Winnipeg in Canada is a bitterly cold −10° F. Siberia's steppes have hot summers and cold winters, too.

Steppes and prairies receive low rainfall. Many places get only 12–20 inches a year. Most falls in summer, when winds bring moist air from the sea. Much rain falls in early summer thunderstorms. Sometimes huge hailstones flatten the crops.

In winter, winds blow out from the middle of the continents and keep them dry. What little moisture exists falls as snow.

Southern temperate grasslands mostly lie nearer to oceans than do the steppe or prairie of the northern hemisphere. They also have milder winters, and rainfall is spread more evenly throughout the year.

With few trees or mountains to slow moving air, temperate grasslands everywhere are windy. Strong cold winds called *pamperos* sweep over Argentina in spring and summer. Southerly "bursters" can afflict southeast Australia, and Texas has its chilly "northers." In warm months fiercely whirling pillars of air called tornadoes track north across the North American plains, sometimes smashing cars and buildings. Winter blizzards whip up fallen snow in Canada and the northern U.S. and the icy *buran* sweeps through Central Asia. But warm *chinook* winds melt snow when they cross the Rockies and reach the western prairies.

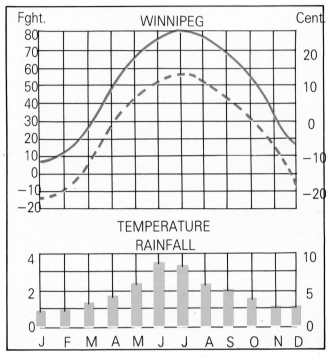

Above The Canadian prairie city Winnipeg has a large annual temperature range and low monthly rainfall.

Below The spinning cloud of a tornado sucks up dusty soil as it tracks across the prairie in Oklahoma.

Yaks protected by their shaggy coats endure intense winter cold on the Central Asian steppe. This scene is in Mongolia.

Storm clouds shed a heavy shower of rain on parched pasture land in Texas. Most rain occurs in summer on the steppes and prairies.

Plant life

Plants that live on steppes or prairies face long, cold, dry winters and hot summers with too little rain to soak the soil thoroughly. Woody plants cannot survive outside moist river valleys. But low, soft-stemmed flowering plants with shallow roots quickly suck up moisture after rain. Annual plants sprout from seeds, make flowers and seeds, and die within one year. Perennial plants live several years, producing leaves and flowers that wither as soil dries up.

Perennial grasses have creeping underground stems called rhizomes that give off roots and shoots called tillers. Tillers produce long, flat, blade-shaped leaves and feathery flower heads. A flower head is made of many spikelets. Each spikelet has scaly leaves and several flowers. Each flower has stamens that produce pollen, stigmas that catch pollen blown about by the wind, and an ovary where pollen fertilizes seeds.

If grazing creatures nibble off the leaves, new side shoots sprout to take their place. Then tillers of fine grasses knit together in a grassy carpet called a sward. Coarser grasses form dense clumps called tussocks.

The grass of the temperate regions is shorter than tropical savanna grass. Mid-high grasses, up to 35 inches tall, thrive near woodlands. The shortest grasses, less than six inches high, occur in arid grasslands.

The grassy plains have fewer kinds of flowers than mountain pastures, but they are often quite colorful. In spring the land is bright blue-green with new grass and sprinkled with the flowers from bulbs. In summer, grass produces feathery spikes and turns yellow as it dies. Now the clovers and other members of the pea family bloom. In autumn the land is yellow with dead grasses and yellow daisies. Only in winter do the plains look drab.

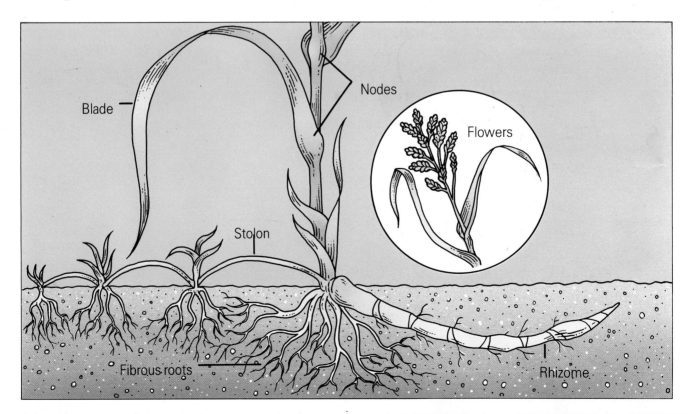

Blade

Nodes

Flowers

Stolon

Fibrous roots

Rhizome

Left Tussocks are dense clumps of coarse grasses. Coarse grasses may form tussocks in places as different from one another as swampy soils and semi-deserts.

Below These three flowers bring color to grassy lands of North America. The pasque flower (prairie crocus) blooms in early spring, the lily and the rose flower later.

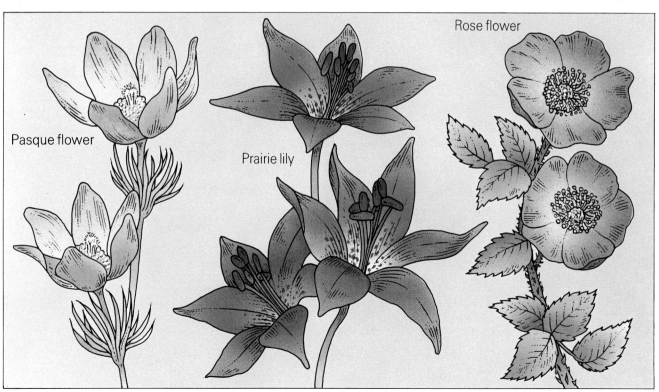

Pasque flower

Prairie lily

Rose flower

Animal life

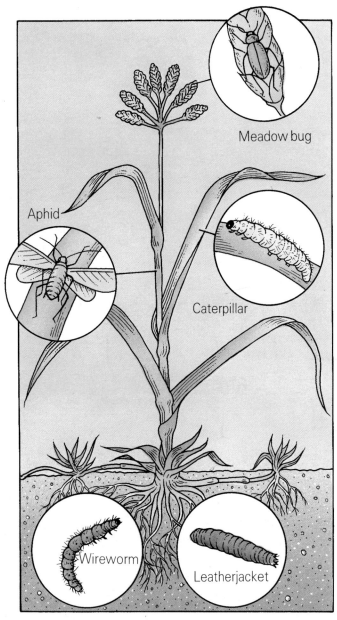

Meadow bug

Aphid

Caterpillar

Wireworm

Leatherjacket

Above Various parts of this grass are eaten by different insects. The wireworm is a larva of the click beetle. The leatherjacket is a crane-fly larva.

Right Kangaroos are Australia's counterparts of the bison and horses that once roamed northern grasslands.

Countless large and small creatures live on the grassy plains. Many feed on grass or other soft-stemmed plants.

Different kinds of insects eat different parts of a grass plant. Grubs of flies and beetles eat roots underground. Aphids suck juices from the stems. Grasshoppers and caterpillars feed on the leaves. Certain bugs prefer the flower heads.

The grass is food for mammals, too. Most temperate grasslands are inhabited by rabbits or hares, and teem with little rodents. All these creatures crop grass with teeth that cut like chisels. The Eurasian steppes are home for gerbils, hamsters, mice, and *susliks* – ground squirrels. North American grasslands have mice, rats, ground squirrels, and prairie dogs. The larger rodents of the pampas are the cavies, chinchillas, and viscachas. Australian grasslands accommodate rat kangaroos and also wombats, which resemble tiny bears.

Hawk

Bison

Hare

Pronghorn antelopes

Mouse

Prairie dogs

Large grazing mammals in Australia include kangaroos and wallabies. On South America's grasslands there are guanacos; and bison and pronghorn antelopes are found on North American prairies. The strange-looking saiga antelope roams the steppes of Asia. Birds such as larks and bustards peck at grasses or their seeds.

Almost all these herbivores (plant-eaters) in turn are food for other animals. Hunting wasps, small birds called wheatears and pipits, and some small mammals such as shrews and marsupial mice all feed on insects. Snakes, hawks, owls, and foxes hunt rodents, rabbits, and small birds. Larger grazing animals have fewer enemies apart from humans, but wolves once killed off many saiga antelopes.

Most herbivores have some defense against attack. Small mammals dive down burrows. Larger ones escape predators by running or leaping.

Somehow, dwellers on the steppe and prairie survive cold winters and lack of food. Rodents stay in burrows where they eat stored food or hibernate. Larger mammals grow thick coats to keep out the cold. Saiga antelopes wander south to snow-free feeding grounds.

These six kinds of creatures find food and living space on prairies. Rodents such as prairie dogs winter underground. But the large, hardy pronghorns and bison endure all weather in the open. Some of the smaller grass-eating mammals are food for birds of prey.

Life long ago

Long ago all temperate grassland people were wandering hunters, herders, or shepherds. They had to keep on the move in order to find new grazing for the beasts they kept or hunted. Some people still live in this way.

The most famous hunters were the Native Americans who roamed the prairies. Blackfoot and other tribes killed pronghorn antelopes and the big meaty ox-like bison often called buffaloes. Bands of them drove bison herds over cliffs or into snowdrifts, then killed them with arrows, lances, stones, and clubs. About a century ago they also were using rifles.

These people ate a lot of bison meat. From bison skins they made long winter robes, shirts, leggings, moccasins, bags, and coverings for tepees.

Indian hunters traveled light. They carried possessions on their backs, or on a travois. This was a pair of poles, with one end hitched to a dog or horse; the other end dragged on the ground.

On the South American pampas, Indians hunted other animals, and gathered roots and berries. Australian Aborigines were also hunter-gatherers. New Zealand's Maori farmed but also killed big flightless birds called moas, which are now extinct.

Meanwhile nomadic Kazak, Mongol, and other tribes roamed Central Asia, seeking pasture for their flocks and herds. Sheep provided milk and wool. From goats came supple leather. Camels and horses served as beasts of burden, and horses gave meat and milk.

From wool or skins grassland people fashioned padded coats, thick woolen trousers, and tall leather boots. Woolen felt covered the domed roofs and upright walls of their windproof tents, called *yurts*. In winter, some tribes built homes made of turf to keep out the bitter cold.

Bantu cattle herders still roam parts of the high veld of South Africa and Lesotho. But many Bantu settled in farm valleys long ago.

Left This photograph gives an idea of the shape and size of yurts put up by Kazak people in Afghanistan. Ropes help to hold in place the light coverings of walls and dome-shaped roofs.

Below More than a century ago, the North American prairies held many encampments like this. The tall, light tents are tepees. These could be easily dismantled, then carried far across the plains by dogs or horses. (Horses first arrived with settlers from Europe.)

Opening up the steppes and prairies

In the early 1800s few people lived on the world's great temperate plains. Yet these almost empty grasslands were suitable for raising sheep or cattle, or for growing crops. Some countries badly needed this extra food, for their populations were multiplying fast. From European cities poor emigrants began swarming out into the pampas, prairies, steppes, veld, and southern downs to turn them into farms and ranches.

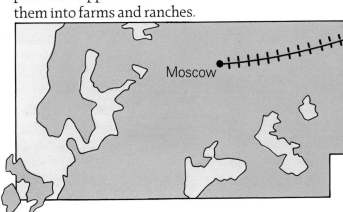

The Trans-Siberian Railroad

N

Moscow

Ulan Bator

Vladivostock

Peking

Canton

Above Begun in 1891, the Trans-Siberian Railroad opened up the vast steppes of Siberia to settlers.

Villages and towns sprang up where railroads spread across the almost empty plains of Canada and the United States. This print shows a scene in 1868.

Some settlers claimed enormous areas of land. But they faced three problems. First, how could they cultivate or ranch huge pieces of open land? Second, how could they bring water to crops or cattle in areas with little rain? Lastly, even if they could produce huge quantities of food, how would they send it to cities located several thousand miles away?

By the early 1900s, new inventions were overcoming all these snags in many places. Tractors and other farm machines helped a few workers to plow, sow seeds, and harvest crops in the very largest fields. Barbed wire enabled cattle farmers to fence off huge ranches to stop cattle from straying.

Obtaining water became easier. Wind pumps sucked up water trapped deep underground. Dams stored river water, and canals and ditches carried it to thirsty land.

Newly opened railroads and roads made it quicker and easier to move grain or meat to cities. As railroads spread through North America cowboys no longer had to drive herds hundreds of miles to reach the nearest railhead. Then, too, big steamships began speeding foods in bulk to countries overseas.

Canning and freezing prevented meat from going bad on long voyages. In 1877 the S.S. *Paraguay* shipped 5,500 frozen mutton carcasses to France from Argentina. Ever since, ships have been carrying frozen beef and lamb from the southern hemisphere to countries far away on the other side of the world.

Below Artesian wells like this yield water for some grassland settlements. The water spurts up under pressure from an aquifer, or water-bearing bed of rock, trapped between impermeable rocks. Underground water not trapped under pressure can be pumped up to the surface.

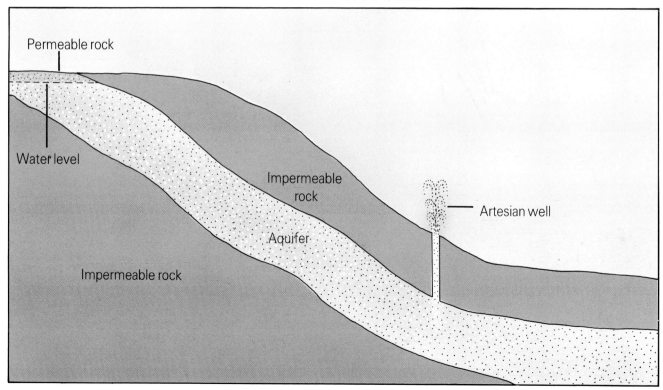

Grassland settlements today

The changes described on pages 18 and 19 have hugely altered temperate grasslands and their inhabitants.

Vast farms with fences and irrigation canals cover most of what was once wild grassland. A few species of domesticated plants and animals have replaced the many kinds that once lived here. People of European descent outnumber the original inhabitants. Even large farms need few farm workers so large tracts of temperate grassland are still thinly peopled.

Where hunters and herders once roamed, farming families now live in comfortable houses. Where horsemen once galloped over trackless land, cars, trucks, buses, and even private planes carry country people and their produce to the nearest town or city. Here farmers can sell their crops and in some places send their children to school.

Life is not the same today on grasslands everywhere. In North America, many farmers own their land. But in the U.S.S.R. and Mongolia most country people work on farms belonging to the government. An average Mongolian collective farm covers 32,000 acres. That makes it about 90 times larger than a typical farm in the Midwest. Collective farms are the world's largest.

Of course not everyone works at raising crops or animals on the land where temperate grasslands stood. Many people live and work in the stores or offices of towns and cities that have grown there. Most Argentinians live in Buenos Aires or other cities and towns that sprawl out into the pampa. In South Africa workers mine under the high veld for gold, diamonds, or other minerals. In fact, South Africa's main mining, manufacturing, and trading centers are on the high veld.

Above Huge tractor trailers like this one in Australia take cattle, sheep, or crops in bulk and quickly from farms to far off cities.

Right Tractors help workers to cultivate huge fields in northern China. Such communist countries have immense collective farms.

Left A sea of grass surrounds the buildings of a lonely ranch near the middle of Montana.

Plants and farming

Temperate grasslands have become the world's bread baskets. Farmers have mostly plowed them up and sown the land with cereals or fodder crops for animals.

Cereals are cultivated grasses with large seeds that we can cook and eat. Cereals provide such foods as bread, cakes, cornflakes, and oatmeal. Temperate grassland soils and soils cleared of temperate forests now produce wheat, corn, barley, oats, and rye. Between them, these cereals yield the equivalent of a ton of grain a year for every four people on earth.

Wheat is the world's largest food crop. It grows best on heavy soil in lands with warm, dry summers. The United States, U.S.S.R., and China are the chief wheat-producing nations.

The world's largest crop of corn comes from the United States' Corn Belt, east of the Ohio River. Here spring moisture and hot summers help the plants to sprout and ripen.

Barley needs less warmth than corn or wheat. The United States, U.S.S.R., and Canada are among the largest crop producers.

Oats and rye thrive in cool summers. They are widely grown in northern Europe, and the U.S.S.R. has the largest crops of both.

Not all of these plants are grown for us to eat. Much barley goes to make malt used in beer and whisky. All five cereals also are fed to farm animals. Most North American corn ends up that way.

Some plants are grown only as fodder. Meadows created by farmers often are sown with rye-grass, a rich source of food for sheep and cattle. Another feed crop is lucerne, or alfalfa. Farmers take up to four cuts a year, and lucerne grows well in drought – its roots can probe down 25 ft. to reach moisture. Then, too, its roots enrich the soil with nitrogen. Lucerne shares this useful work with clover, vetch, and lupine. All these so-called legumes help restore lost fertility to soil.

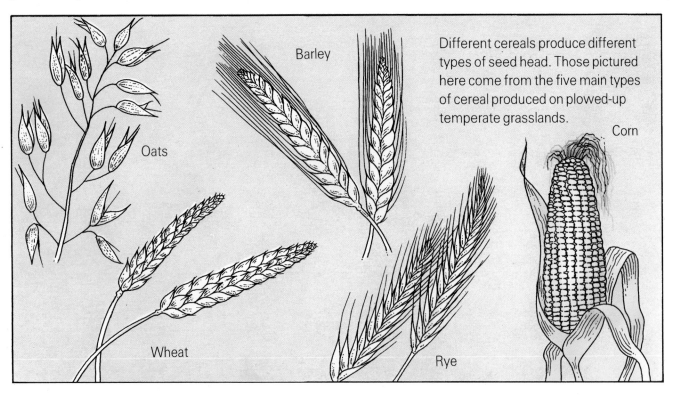

Barley

Oats

Different cereals produce different types of seed head. Those pictured here come from the five main types of cereal produced on plowed-up temperate grasslands.

Corn

Wheat

Rye

Combine harvesters reap wheat from grain fields stretching to the skyline and beyond. This scene comes from the United States, one of the largest wheat producers in the world.

Below Giant silos store grain grown on the pampas in Argentina. Trucks help to give an idea of the silos' size.

Farm animals

Tame sheep and cattle graze the grassy plains where big, wild mammals once roamed. People value sheep and cattle because their special stomachs help them turn grass into large quantities of substances we need. Between them, sheep and cattle give us meat, milk, wool, and leather.

Domesticated sheep come from agile ancestors that ranged the grassy mountain slopes of southwest Asia. Tame cattle come from the wild cattle that once roamed the forest glades of Asia and Europe. From those lean, wild animals, selective breeding produced the docile, meaty beasts that we see today.

Below Hereford bulls are bred for beef as they yield the most meat for the lowest cost.

Above A motorcycling farmer tends Friesian cattle thriving on the lush grass of a meadow in New Zealand.

For every 100 people in the world there are about six cattle. Temperate grasslands of the United States, U.S.S.R., Argentina, and Brazil are among the top ten producing regions.

There are two main types of cattle. Beef cattle have stocky bodies with broad backs. They include the Aberdeen Angus, Beef Shorthorn, Charolais, Hereford, and Highland breeds. Beef cattle are bred to yield the most meat for the lowest cost. They can graze grassland too poor for dairy herds. Dairy breeds are leaner than beef cattle, but have roomy stomachs and convert much grass into milk. Dairy cattle include the Ayrshire, Friesian, Guernsey, and Jersey breeds. Dairy cattle fed on lush pastures produce the highest yields.

The world holds about half as many sheep as cattle. Australia raises more sheep than any other nation. Other top producing regions include the temperate grasslands of China, Turkey, India, New Zealand, Britain, South Africa, and Iran.

Sheep are bred chiefly for meat and wool. Most sheep can live off drier, poorer grass than that required by cattle. But highland breeds with thick coats like the Scottish Blackface can survive colder winters than the Romney from the English lowlands. These breeds and cross-breeds from the British Isles now thrive on grassy hills and plains of many lands. Some other European breeds like the fine wool-coated Merino sheep, which first came from Spain, also thrive in temperate grasslands.

Merino sheep pause for wayside grazing as their flock ambles down a sunlit road in Victoria, Australia.

The savannas

Hot grasslands, or savannas, are tropical plains or plateaus with grass and scattered shrubs and trees. Most savannas tend to have taller grasses and more trees than you find on pampas, steppes, or prairies. But grass is shorter and trees are scarcer on the driest land.

Most savannas lie north and south of the tropical rainforests that straddle the equator. Beyond some savannas lie hot deserts. East and west, savanna may be rimmed by mountains, sea, or forest.

South America has several big savanna areas. North of the Amazon forests the *llanos* or plains of the Orinoco River basin cover an area of Colombia and Venezuela the size of Texas or France. There are few trees, except where palms line river banks. Similar grasslands sprawl from southeast Venezuela through southern Guyana. Far larger and more wooded, the *campos* take up most of the Brazilian Highlands south of the Amazon forests.

Above Ducks fly over cattle standing in a muddy, drying pool on the grassy plains of Venezuela.

Below Giraffes in Kenya loom above savanna trees and grasses. More savanna covers the rift valley beyond.

Here lie huge tracts of grassy parkland mixed with clumps of scrubby trees. Along the Upper Paraguay River is *pantanal* – a kind of wet savanna grassland mixed with palm trees.

The world's largest savanna forms a long, broad belt that takes up nearly half of Africa. From the Atlantic shores of West Africa, this belt thrusts east across the continent to the Sudan. Then it runs south through East Africa. From Mozambique on the Indian Ocean, the belt heads west through Zambia and Angola back to the Atlantic Ocean.

As you leave Africa's tropical rainforests, you pass from woods with grassy patches, through savanna with tall grass and scattered trees, to drier thornbush with short grass.

Drier parts of India's great Deccan Plateau rank among the world's savannas. Also, a large savanna belt with low trees and drought-resistant shrubs crosses Australia north and east of the great, hot central deserts.

Seen from a mountain top, grassland and semi-desert sprawl across the hot, flat heart of Australia.

Weather and climate

Savanna weather is warm or hot in every month. After a long, dry winter many savannas have intense dry heat, followed by a short and rainy summer.

These changes follow the sun as it swings north and south of the equator. For the sun's shift moves great air masses that bring rain or drought. In winter, a mass of warm, dry sinking air covers some savanna lands. Others lie beneath steady trade winds that have blown far overland and lost their moisture on the way. Either way, for months the air stays dry, skies are clear, and the weather grows extremely hot. In summer, moist, hot air moves in from the equator. Heavy showers begin to fall. The rainy season has arrived.

Savanna lands with a dry overland winter wind and a moist summer wind are said to have a monsoon climate. The word monsoon comes from the Arabic *mausim*, meaning season. In lands with monsoon climates winds blow from opposite directions at different times of year.

Although most savannas lie in the tropics, not all are equally dry. For instance, some Australian savannas get a mere 18 inches of rain a year, while moist African savannas can receive three times as much as that. In South America heavy downpours even flood the llanos and pantanal. But everywhere rainfall tends to dwindle as you travel farther from the equator.

Most savannas average daily summer temperatures above 80° F, and winter temperatures above 65° F. But average temperatures vary less from month to month than between day and night. In the southern Sudan the difference between the hottest and coolest month is only 10° F but the difference between the coldest time of night and the warmest time of day is never less than 20° F. During the night the temperature cools down very quickly when there are no clouds to trap heat near the ground. The day's heat then escapes into the atmosphere.

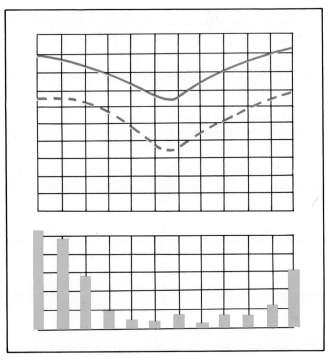

Above Monthly maximum temperatures stay high, but rain is seasonal in the Australian savanna town Cloncurry.

Below Green grass and storm-soaked ground show the rainy season has arrived in the south of the Sudan.

Right Inky sky and green-tinged ground mark the onset of the rains in northern Australia. The mud "spikes" are termite mounds.

Below In the dry season this Brazilian savanna is a sea of sun-dried grasses, with mostly leafless shrubs and trees.

Plant life

This acacia blooms before its leaves appear. Long thorns help to protect both from browsing animals.

Different parts of a savanna have different plants. An African journey north from the equator shows how and why they vary.

Just beyond the rainforest is a mixture of forest and savanna. Grass twice as high as a human surrounds isolated clumps of forest trees. Unbroken forest once flourished in the moist soil. But most trees have been burned down by farmers or herders. Now only fire-resistant trees and shrubs survive among the grasses.

Next comes wooded savanna – a drier park-like area of tall grasses with low, scattered fire-resistant trees and, in places, shrubby undergrowth. Strong winds and nibbling giraffes have shaped many trees like umbrellas, though sharp spines give some protection from big herbivores.

Farther on you reach the dry savanna. This is drier and hotter than wooded savanna. Its chief plants are short grasses and scattered trees and shrubs that can survive long droughts.

The wooded and grassy steppe regions are even drier still. Tussocks of short, wiry grass and thickets of low thorn trees grow here.

Lastly comes the dry steppe of the Sahel. This great belt just south of the Sahara Desert supports only scattered tufts of grass and thorny bushes, with patches of bare ground between.

Somehow, savanna plants survive drought and fire. In the long dry season, grasses, bulbs, and tubers die down yet stay alive below the soil. Some acacia trees shed leaves to reduce their need for moisture. Baobab trees store water in their fat trunks. As summer rains arrive, leaves sprout, flowers bloom, and the brown land turns bright green.

Trees with tough corky bark escape dry-season fires. Dead leaf sheaths shelter grass shoots from the flames. Changes in air moisture help some fallen grass seeds to make their way safely into the soil before the fires break out. This ensures that new grass will grow again.

A baobab tree manages to survive months of hot, dry weather by shedding leaves and storing water in its fat, fire-resistant trunk.

Animal life

Savannas teem with animals. Billions of termites, locusts, and other insects feed on vegetation. There are vast flocks of finches, budgerigars, or other seed-eating birds. Small mammals like Australia's native cats and Africa's mongooses prey on small game, from insects to snakes and lizards.

But the best-known savanna dwellers are the big game of Africa. Large plant-eaters include elephants, hippopotamuses, rhinoceroses, zebras, and dozens of kinds of antelope from the eland weighing about a ton to the pygmy antelope which is no bigger than a dog.

Many African species can share the same area because each eats different food so there is enough for all. Zebras prefer tall fibrous grasses. Gnus like shorter grasses. Gazelles mainly eat low grass and hartebeests crop dryish stalks that other herbivores reject. The gerenuk, a long-necked antelope, stands on hind legs to browse on low branches. Giraffes feed among the treetops.

Many of these herbivores migrate with summer rains that spread fresh new vegetation across the plains. Antelopes and zebras roam in herds for protection.

The ostrich, the biggest bird on earth, roams the African plains, unable to fly. It looks rather like two other big flightless grassland birds: Australia's emu and Argentina's rhea. All three are known as ratites, from *ratis*, the Latin word for raft. Ratites have a flat, raft-shaped breastbone without a jutting keel to anchor flight muscles. But this similarity could be coincidence. Ratites might not be close relatives at all.

The main threat to Africa's big herbivores comes from lions, cheetahs, leopards, hyenas, and hunting

An emu photographed running at high speed. Long, sprinter's legs make up for the inability to fly.

Lion   Ostrich

Zebras

Above Wild budgerigars flock to drink at a savanna pool in Australia. Some flocks number in the thousands.

dogs. Lions creep up through long grass, then rush upon their prey. But a pack of hunting dogs will chase a wildebeest far across the plains. When a killer has eaten, scavenging jackals, vultures, and marabou storks move in to finish off the feast.

Vultures

Giraffe

Gnus

Thomson's gazelle

Banded mongoose

Beetle

Old ways of life

Our early ancestors most likely came from the East African savanna. Here lived the australopithecines, whose name means southern apes. These ape-like creatures left their bones and footprints in East Africa more than three million years ago. Approximately two million years ago they seemingly had given rise to *Homo habilis*, or handy man. This small, more human-looking creature made stone tools and simple huts. *Homo habilis* ate wild roots and fruits and stole meat from the bodies of savanna creatures killed by lions or other carnivores. By one and a half million years ago *Homo habilis* had evolved to larger, brainier *Homo erectus* meaning upright man. This early big-game hunter of the Old Stone Age spread from Africa to Europe and Asia. By 200,000 years ago, *Homo erectus* had produced our species, *Homo sapiens* or wise man.

These modern humans were hunting and gathering wild foods on the savannas of Africa, India, and Australia 40,000 years ago. Later, hunters reached South America's great grasslands. Everywhere, small bands armed with spears or arrows killed antelopes, kangaroos, or other game. A few Australian Aborigines still hunt and forage like that – living a mostly nomadic life.

Below Masai herdsmen and cattle stand before the ring of mud-dung houses that forms a Masai village. Cattle provide the Masai with meat, hides, and milk.

Above Aboriginal hunter-gatherers like this man were Australia's only inhabitants until 200 years ago.

Below In India oxen drag simple plows across the land as they have for several thousand years.

But 13,000 years ago ways of life were changing on the African savanna. East African people had begun keeping cattle for meat, milk, and hides. These nomads wandered with their herds from one pasture to another.

About 7,000 years ago there were African savanna farmers, too. They began growing crops and building mud homes in villages. They sowed small plots with millet, sorghum, and other food plants. When the soil became exhausted, the farmers simply moved elsewhere.

These New Stone Age ways of life survive almost unchanged among peoples like Kenya's Masai herders and Zambia's Bemba. However, the hunter-gatherers have vanished from savannas almost everywhere.

New ways of life

Above A Kenyan worker hangs out sisal fibers to dry Sisal is an agave plant used for making twine.

Below Three crops grown on savanna lands. Tobacco is cultivated for its leaves, cotton for its fluffy seed fibers, and the peanut plant for its underground seeds.

By the early 1900s settlers from Europe and the United States were moving into the savanna lands. Ambitious people established mighty ranches and plantations. Unlike native savanna people, the owners of these great estates wanted to produce much more than they could eat. They aimed to sell the surplus abroad.

Savanna settlers faced the same problems as the pioneers who opened up the temperate grasslands (see page 18) and there were extra snags. Crops and breeds of cattle suitable for cooler climates died or sickened in the tropics. Tropical diseases such as sleeping sickness struck down Europeans or their animals in much of Africa. Everywhere, flies attacked the cattle's hides, and swarms of locusts or grain-eating finches sometimes devastated crops.

Bit by bit most problems have been largely overcome. Modern medicines and pesticides have made large areas of savanna healthier for people and their crops and cattle. Irrigation schemes allow some crops to grow where there is little rain. Roads and railroads help farmers transport their produce to the coasts.

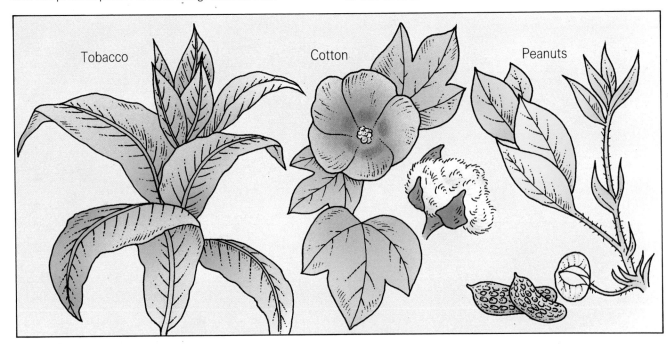

Tobacco   Cotton   Peanuts

Ranchers now keep beef cattle that resist heat and insects and thrive on pastures too poor for European breeds. India's Brahman cattle and the part-Brahman part-shorthorn Santa Gertrudis breed flourish on South America's llanos and pantanal, and in Australia's Northern Territory. In Africa, crossing local cattle with European beef and dairy breeds also has produced disease-resistant

beasts that can cope with the heat.

Now, too, savanna plantations are successfully producing cash crops, which means crops the grower sells instead of eating. Great tracts of land in Africa are used for growing cotton, peanuts, sisal, and tobacco. Vast fields of corn and rice have spread into the campos of Brazil.

Yet drought, tropical disease, or travel problems leave immense savanna tracts untouched by modern farms or ranches. Many Africans still hoe small plots of land or wander with their flocks or herds across dry grasslands on the desert edge.

Cowhands with steers at a Brazilian cattle market. Shoulder humps and floppy ears show these beasts are Brahmans, a breed resisting heat and tropical disease.

The fragile soil

Soil is the most valuable ingredient in any grassland. Remove the soil and you are left with a desert.

Soil forms slowly, over thousands of years. First, weathering breaks rock into tiny pieces. Tiny plants grow on these fragments. When the plants die, bacteria break them down into substances that nourish larger plants with longer roots. Meanwhile, tiny creatures feed upon the dead and living plants. In time decayed plants, animals, and animal droppings form a dark, fertile substance called humus. Humus mixed with rock fragments makes up soil.

Different climates produce different soils. In fairly dry temperate grasslands there is too little rain to wash humus deep down. It forms a dark, rich layer just below the surface. In Russian, the name of this soil is *chernozem* which means "black earth." A great belt of black earth underlies the steppes of eastern Europe and central Asia. Similar dark soils take up parts of the North American prairies, Argentine pampas, and Australian downs. These regions of black earths are among the world's great wheatlands.

Somewhat moister temperate climates produce dark brown prairie soils. These form inside continents, where the year's rainfall is 25–40 inches. Rain washes some nutrients deep down, but enough remain to nourish tall grasses. The "corn" belt in the United States and parts of eastern Europe have prairie soils.

Climates somewhat drier than those producing chernozem lead to the chestnut-colored soils to be found in the southern U.S.S.R., the High Plains east of the Rocky Mountains, and parts of the South African veld and Argentine pampas.

Tropical savanna climates create red earths. Their rusty color comes from water joining iron in the ground. Heat and moisture help to break up rocks as much as 50 feet deep. Rainwater washes some plant foods far down, but crops grow well at first. Red earths cover savanna plateaus in Brazil, Guyana, East Africa, and southern India.

All these soils are frail and easily destroyed.

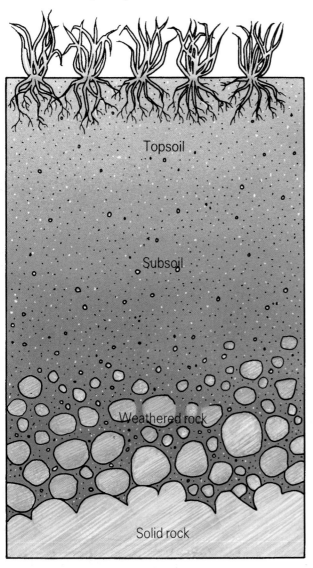

Topsoil

Subsoil

Weathered rock

Solid rock

Left A section through soil – a product of weathered rock and the remains of living things.

Right Sections through four grassland soils are linked to a map showing the areas where they occur.

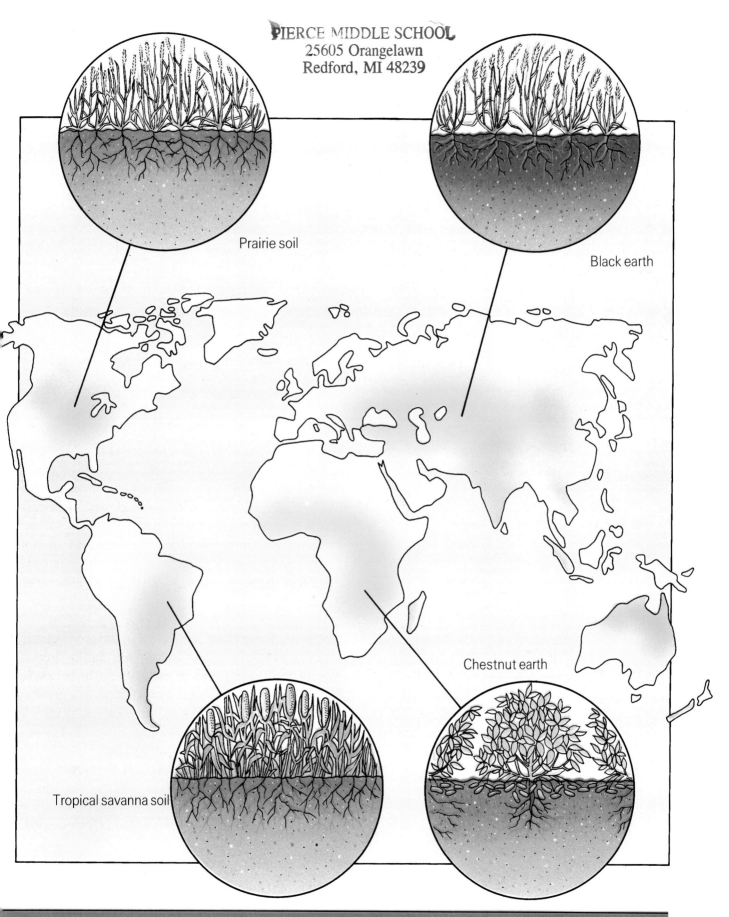

Prairie soil

Black earth

Tropical savanna soil

Chestnut earth

Misusing grasslands

Humans have been damaging wild grasslands for centuries. The damage happened slowly while few people inhabited the prairies and savannas. However, since 1900 damage has speeded up as multiplying populations have tried to tame the plains. Animals, plants, and soils all suffer.

By 1890, hunters already had killed off North America's great bison herds. Today, African poachers are wiping out the world's last black rhinoceroses. Most big African animals could disappear as farmers and herders take over the savanna.

Too much burning and too many livestock have badly damaged the wild plants of dry African grassland. Where cattle and sheep have eaten all the grass, only scrawny shrubs will grow. Where goats and camels eat what remains, the ground grows bare. Introducing foreign plants and animals also can damage native vegetation. In Australia rabbits destroyed vast pastures, and prickly pear cacti made much land unusable.

Replacing native plants with crops brings problems, too. Pests and weeds multiply, and disease suddenly may attack one kind of crop grown on the same field year after year.

Below A fence in Texas divides grazed land from ungrazed land. On dry soil like this overgrazing is liable to destroy the vegetation altogether.

The greatest danger comes from overusing the soil. Two ways of doing this are by plowing up very dry soil and by growing crops without adding fertilizer. Grasslands also are damaged by cattle overgrazing dry savanna and by people burning cow dung as fuel instead of leaving it to enrich the soil. Overuse makes soil infertile.

All this translates into fewer plants and more bare earth. Bare soil holds little moisture. Without soil moisture, rainfall dwindles, so dry lands get drier still. The plants that survive are starved of nourishment and water. Their weak roots no longer can grip the soil. Rain or wind can then wash or blow the soil away. In the 1930s soil erosion turned much of the North American prairies into a barren Dust Bowl. Since the 1960s the Sahara Desert has invaded Africa's dry Sahel region. Here, thirst and hunger have killed many thousands of people and their cattle.

Above Barren gullies near Kenya's Lake Baringo show where rain has eaten deeply into soil laid bare by overgrazing. Here, overused savanna is fast becoming desert.

Right Hungry cattle that have eaten all their grass soon may grow thin and die. Scenes like this in Ethiopia occur when new grass fails to grow. But land shortage forces herders to keep their beasts in a countryside that sometimes suffers drought.

Saving grasslands

Much can be done to save threatened grassland soils, plants, and animals.

Farmers can avoid plowing prairies so dry that loosened topsoil soon blows away. Adding fertilizer helps soil produce crops year after year. Digging irrigation ditches and canals can bring water to thirsty plants. But on dry savanna, it costs less to grow drought-resistant grains like millet and sorghum.

Planting hedges or shelter belts of trees on plains slows down the wind. This helps prevent soil from being blown away. People have begun planting trees and shrubs around Sahelian cities including Ouagadougou in Burkina Faso, and Niamey in Niger. Here, acacias and certain other trees grow quickly even in dry ground. After a few years people can safely cut some down to burn or feed to cattle.

Overgrazed vegetation will recover if it is fenced off and cattle, sheep, and goats are kept out. After a few years some can be let in again. One problem is where to put them to feed before the vegetation has regrown.

A new invention called land imprinting makes it easier for grassland to regrow on dry soils open to the wind. A roller with special knobs presses artificial hoofprints into the ground. Rainwater collecting in the prints helps seeds to grow.

There are several ways of saving wild grassland creatures threatened with extinction. Governments limit how many creatures hunters are allowed to kill each year. Governments also set aside large areas of grassland as reserves. Here, game wardens try to protect wild animals from farmers, herders, and poachers. Game reserves in nations such as Kenya earn valuable money for their countries from visitors who come to see big wild creatures roaming free.

As the world's fast-increasing human population needs more food, saving grasslands from overuse gets harder. But if we don't succeed, people everywhere might one day suffer famine.

Above: Stone terraces slow rainfall run-off, helping check soil erosion here in Ethiopia's highlands.

Left Tourists on safari in East Africa get a rare glimpse of a leopard from the safety of their minibus.

Right: Armed guards set out by truck to protect big game from poachers in Kenya's Tsavo National Park.

Glossary

Aborigines People native to a place, unlike people who have moved in from outside. The term is especially used to describe the original inhabitants of Australia.

Annual A plant that only lives for one year or one season.

Australopithecines Prehistoric ape-like creatures of Africa. One kind probably gave rise to humans.

Bison A wild, ox-like creature with a big head, short horns, shaggy mane, and humped shoulders.

Black earths Dark, fertile soils including *chernozem*.

Campos Tropical grasslands of Brazil.

Cereals Cultivated grasses with big edible grains, or the grains themselves.

Chernozem Dark, fertile soil found in the steppes.

Collective farm Many small farms lumped together as one huge farm under government control.

Downs Rolling treeless uplands.

Dust bowl Land suffering long droughts and dust storms.

Fodder Food fed to horses, sheep, or cattle.

Game reserve Land set aside for wildlife.

Guanaco A South American mammal related to the camel but without a hump.

Humus Dark, fertile material in soil. It contains rotted plant and animal substances.

Land imprinting Pressing artificial "hoofprints" in dry soil to help grass seed to grow.

Llanos Tropical grasslands in northern South America.

Locust Any of several kinds of large grasshopper. Locust swarms devour all vegetation in their path.

Lucerne (alfalfa) A deep-rooted plant of the pea family, grown as fodder and to enrich the soil.

Moor Rolling open land, often with boggy soil and grasses.

Pamir High plateau grasslands of Central Asia.

Pampas Temperate grasslands of South America.

Pantanal Tropical grassland liable to flooding, found along the Upper Paraguay River in South America.

Patana Mountain grassland of Sri Lanka.

Perennial A plant that lives for several years.

Poacher A person who illegally hunts on someone else's property.

Prairies The vast grasslands of North America.

Pronghorn A North American mammal resembling an antelope.

Puna High plateau grassland of Bolivia.

Pusztas Grassy plains of Hungary.

Red earths Reddish soils of the savannas.

Rhizome An underground stem.

Sahel The great belt of dry grassland south of the Sahara Desert.

Savanna Tropical grassland.

Sisal A Mexican plant whose fiber is used for making rope.

Sleeping sickness A serious disease spread by the tsetse fly in parts of Africa.

Soil The loose upper layer of the ground in which plants grow.

Soil erosion The wearing away of soil by wind or running water.

Spikelet Part of the flowerhead of a grass.

Steppes Vast dry grasslands of Southeast Europe and Central Asia.

Tiller A shoot sprouting from the base of a plant.

Yurt A round, domed tent covered with felt and built by Central Asian tribes.

Left A tourist perched on a jeep roof enjoys the sights and sounds of an African savanna sunset.

Further reading

Clive Catchpole *Grasslands* (Dial Books, for Young Readers 1984).
Michael Cuisin *Desert Dwellers* (Silver Burdett Press 1987).
Catherine Horton *Grasslands and People* (Silver Burdett Press 1982).
Daniel Alibert-Kouraguine *Prairie Dwellers* (Silver Burdett Press 1983).

James P. Rowan *Prairies & Grasslands* (Children Pr. 1983).
Louis Sabin *Grasslands* (Troll Assocs. 1984).
The Living World of Animals edited by L. Harrison Matthews and Richard Carrington (Reader's Digest 1970).

Picture acknowledgments

The publishers would like to thank the following for allowing their photographs to be reproduced in this book: Biofotos 5, 26 (above); J. Allen Cash 9 (right); Bruce Coleman 7, 9 (left), 20, 25, 29 (inset), 30, 32, 33, 41 (above), 42 (left); Geoscience 26 (below) inset; Eric and David Hosking 43; Hutchison 11 (inset), 21 (above and below), 28–9, 35 (below), 41 (below), 42 (right); Frank Lane 10, 34; Peter Newark's Western Americana 18; Oxford Scientific Films 11, 36, 40; Picturepoint 23; Wayland 13, 23 (inset), 24 (above); ZEFA 6, 8, 14, 27, 31, 35 (above), 37, 44. Cover illustration by Stephen Lings. All other illustrations by John Yates. Front cover photos ZEFA; back cover GeoScience Features.

Index

574.5   Lambert, David C1
LAM
          Grasslands

$14.98

DATE			
NO 02'90			
JA 21'93			
DE 2 '9			

© THE BAKER & TAYLOR CO.